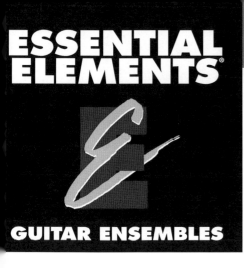

ESSENTIAL ELEMENTS®

GUITAR ENSEMBLES

POPULAR SONGS

CONTENTS

Arrangements by Mark Phillips

ISBN 978-1-4950-9956-4

Visit Hal Leonard Online at
www.halleonard.com

Contact Us:
Hal Leonard
7777 West Bluemound Road
Milwaukee, WI 53213
Email: info@halleonard.com

In Europe contact:
Hal Leonard Europe Limited
Distribution Centre, Newmarket Road
Bury St Edmunds, Suffolk, IP33 3YB
Email: info@halleonardeurope.com

In Australia contact:
Hal Leonard Australia Pty. Ltd.
4 Lentara Court
Cheltenham, Victoria, 3192 Australia
Email: info@halleonard.com.au

ALL ABOUT THAT BASS

Words and Music by Kevin Kadish and Meghan Trainor

BOULEVARD OF BROKEN DREAMS

Words by Billie Joe
Music by Green Day

CHASING CARS

Words and Music by Gary Lightbody, Tom Simpson, Paul Wilson, Jonathan Quinn and Nathan Connolly

HEY THERE DELILAH

Words and Music by Tom Higgenson

I WILL WAIT

Words and Music by Mumford & Sons

Gtr. III: Drop D tuning:
(low to high) D-A-D-G-B-E

LONELY BOY

Words and Music by Dan Auerbach, Patrick Carney and Brian Burton

POKER FACE

Words and Music by Stefani Germanotta and RedOne

RIDE

Words and Music by Tyler Joseph

ROLLING IN THE DEEP

Words and Music by Adele Adkins and Paul Epworth

SEVEN NATION ARMY

Words and Music by Jack White

SOME NIGHTS

Words and Music by Jeff Bhasker, Andrew Dost, Jack Antonoff and Nate Ruess

STORY OF MY LIFE

Words and Music by Jamie Scott, John Henry Ryan, Julian Bunetta,
Harry Styles, Liam Payne, Louis Tomlinson, Niall Horan and Zain Malik

UPTOWN FUNK

Words and Music by Mark Ronson, Bruno Mars, Philip Lawrence, Jeff Bhasker, Devon Gallaspy, Nicholaus Williams,
Lonnie Simmons, Ronnie Wilson, Charles Wilson, Rudolph Taylor and Robert Wilson

Gtr. III: Drop D tuning:
(low to high) D-A-D-G-B-E

Intro
Moderately

*Double stops in Gtr. II can be played up an octave,
on the 12th and 13th frets of the E and B strings.

Verse
N.C.

**(Muted strums)

**Optional: Include foot stomps
on beats 1 & 3 (next 8 meas.).

Pre-Chorus
N.C.

VIVA LA VIDA

Words and Music by Guy Berryman, Jon Buckland, Will Champion and Chris Martin

SHAPE OF YOU

Words and Music by Ed Sheeran, Kevin Briggs, Kandi Burruss, Tameka Cottle, Steve Mac and Johnny McDaid